ISBN 978-0-243-22219-3
PIBN 10789523

This book is a reproduction of an important historical work. Forgotten Books uses state-of-the-art technology to digitally reconstruct the work, preserving the original format whilst repairing imperfections present in the aged copy. In rare cases, an imperfection in the original, such as a blemish or missing page, may be replicated in our edition. We do, however, repair the vast majority of imperfections successfully; any imperfections that remain are intentionally left to preserve the state of such historical works.

1 MONTH OF
FREE
READING

at
www.ForgottenBooks.com

By purchasing this book you are eligible for one month membership to ForgottenBooks.com, giving you unlimited access to our entire collection of over 700,000 titles via our web site and mobile apps.

To claim your free month visit:
www.forgottenbooks.com/free789523

English
Français
Deutsche
Italiano
Español
Português

www.forgottenbooks.com

Mythology Photography **Fiction**
Fishing Christianity **Art** Cooking
Essays Buddhism Freemasonry
Medicine **Biology** Music **Ancient**
Egypt Evolution Carpentry Physics
Dance Geology **Mathematics** Fitness
Shakespeare **Folklore** Yoga Marketing
Confidence Immortality Biographies
Poetry **Psychology** Witchcraft
Electronics Chemistry History **Law**
Accounting **Philosophy** Anthropology
Alchemy Drama Quantum Mechanics
Atheism Sexual Health **Ancient History**
Entrepreneurship Languages Sport
Paleontology Needlework Islam
Metaphysics Investment Archaeology
Parenting Statistics Criminology
Motivational

DR. WATTS

PLAIN AND EASY

CATECHISMS

FOR

CHILDREN:

TOGETHER WITH A COLLECTION OF

HYMNS AND PRAYERS.

SEVENTH MIDDLETOWN EDITION.

MIDDLETOWN, (CONN.)

PRINTED AND PUBLISHED BY E. & H. CLARK.

1826.

DR. WATTS'

PLAIN AND EASY

CATECHISMS FOR CHILDREN.

------•◉◉•------

FIRST CATECHISM.

OF THE PRINCIPLES OF RELIGION.

Quest. Can you tell me, child, who made you?

Ans. The Great God, who made Heaven and Earth.

Q. What doth God do for you?

A. He keeps me from harm by night and by day, and is always doing me good.

Q. And what must you do for this great God, who is so good to you?

A. I must learn to know him first, and then I must do every thing to please him.

Q. Where doth God teach us to know and to please him?

A. In his holy word which is contained in the Bible.

Q. Have you learned to know who God is?

A. God is a Spirit; and though we cannot see him, yet he sees and knows all things, and he can do all things.

Q. What must you do to please God?

A. I must do my duty both toward God and man.

Q. What is your duty to God?

A. My duty to God is to fear and honour him, to love and serve him, to pray to him, and to praise him.

Q. What is your duty to man?

A. My duty to man is to obey my parents, to speak the truth always, and to be honest and kind to all.

Q. What good do you hope for by seeking to please God?

A. Then I shall be a Child of God, and have God for my Father and Friend for ever.

Q. And what if you do not fear God, nor love him, nor seek to please him?

A. Then I shall be a wicked child, and the great God will be very angry with me.

Q. Why are you afraid of God's anger?

A. Because he can kill my body, and make my soul miserable after my body is dead.

Q. But have you never done any thing to make God angry with you already?

A. Yes; I fear I have too often sinned against God, and deserved his anger.

Q. What do you mean by sinning against God?

A. To sin against God is to do any thing he forbids me, or not to do what he commands me.

Q. And what must you do to be saved from the anger of God which your sins have deserved?

A. I must be sorry for my sins, I must pray to God to forgive me what is past, and serve him better for time to come.

Q. Will God forgive you if you pray for it?

A. I hope he will forgive me, if I trust in his mercy, for the sake of what Jesus Christ has done, and what he has suffered.

Q. Do you know who Jesus Christ is?

A. He is God's own Son, who came from Heaven to save us from our sins, and from God's anger.

Q. What has Christ done towards the saving of men?

A. He obeyed the law of God himself, and has taught us to obey it also.

Q. And what has Christ suffered in order to save men?

A. He died for sinners, who had broken the law of God, & had deserved to die themselves.

Q. Where is Jesus Christ now?

A. He is alive again, and gone to Heaven, to provide a place there for all that serve God and love his Son Jesus.

Q. Can you of yourself love and serve God and Christ?

A. No, I cannot do it of myself, but God will help me by his own Spirit, if I ask him for it.

Q. Will Jesus Christ ever come again?

A. Christ will come again, and call me and

1 *

all the world to account for what we have done.

Q. For what purpose is this account to be given?

A. That the Children of God, as well as the wicked, may all receive according to their works.

Q. What must become of you if you are wicked?

A. If I am wicked, I shall be sent down to everlasting fire in Hell, among wicked and miserable creatures.

Q. And whither shall you go if you are a child of God?

A. If I am a child of God, I shall be taken up to Heaven, and dwell there with God and Christ for ever. *Amen.*

SECOND CATECHISM.

OF THE PRINCIPLES OF RELIGION.

Quest. Dear child do you know what you are?

Ans. I am a creature of God, for he made me, both body and soul.

Q. How do you know you have a soul?

A. Because I find something within me that can think and know, can wish and desire, can rejoice and be sorry, which my body cannot do.

Q. Wherein doth your soul differ further from your body?

A. My body is made of flesh and blood, and it will die: but my soul is a spirit, and it will live after my body is dead.

Q. For what purpose did God make you such a creature, with a body and a soul?

A. To know him and serve him here on earth, that I may dwell with him and be happy hereafter in Heaven.

Q. How must you learn to know God and to serve him?

A. By the holy Scriptures of the Old and New Testament, which are the word of God.

Q. What do the Scriptures teach you of the knowledge of God?

A. The Scriptures teach me what God is in himself, and what he is in relation to us who are his creatures.

Q. Who is God, considered in himself, or in his own nature?

A. God in his own nature is a Spirit, every where present, without beginning and without end, most wise and powerful, most holy and merciful, most just and true.

Q. What is God in relation to us, who are his creatures?

A. As the great God is our Maker, who gave us our being, so he continually preserves us, and does us good: He is our Lord and Ruler now, and he will be our Judge at last.

Q. *And how* o *the Scriptures teach you to serve God?*

A. I must serve God, by keeping all his commandments, that is, by doing every thing that he requires of me, and avoiding every thing that he forbids me.

Q. *What commandments has God given to men?*

A. He gave the law of ten commandments to the Jews in the Old Testament, and they are summed up in two commandments for us in the New Testament.

Q. *Repeat the ten commandments of God, which he gave in the Old Testament—What is the first commandment?*

A. The first commandment is, *Thou shalt have no other Gods before me.*

Q. *What is the second commandment?*

A. The second commandment is, *Thou shalt not make unto thee any graven image, or any likeness of any thing that is in heaven above, or that is in the earth beneath, or that is in the water under the earth. Thou shalt not bow down thyself to them, nor serve them, for I the Lord thy God am a jealous God, visiting the iniquities of the fathers upon the children unto the third and fourth generation of them that hate me; and shewing mercies unto thousands of them that love me and keep my commandments.*

Q. *What is the third commandment?*

A. The third commandment is, *Thou shalt*

not take the name of the Lord thy God in vain, for the Lord will not hold him guiltless that taketh his name in vain.

Q. What is the fourth commandment?

A. The fourth commandment is, *Remember the Sabbath day, to keep it holy. Six days shalt thou labour, and do all thy work; but the seventh day is the Sabbath of the Lord thy God, in it thou shalt not do any work, thou, nor thy son, nor thy daughter, nor thy man servant, nor thy maid servant, nor thy cattle, nor the stranger that is within thy gates; for in six days the Lord made heaven and earth, the sea, and all that in them is, and rested the seventh day, wherefore the Lord blessed the sabbath day, and hallowed it.*

Q. What is the fifth commandment?

A. The fifth commandment is, *Honour thy father and thy mother, that thy days may be long upon the land which the Lord thy God giveth thee.*

Q. What is the sixth commandment?

A. The sixth commandment is, *Thou shalt not kill.*

Q. What is the seventh commandment?

A. The seventh commandment is, *Thou shalt not commit adultery.*

Q. What is the eighth commandment?

A. The eighth commandment is, *Thou shalt not steal.*

Q. What is the ninth commandment?

A. The ninth commandment is, *Thou shalt not bear false witness against thy neighbour.*

Q. What is the tenth commandment ?

A. The tenth commandment is; *Thou shalt not covet thy neighbour's house ; thou shalt not covet thy neighbour's wife, nor his man servant, nor his maid servant, nor his ox, nor his ass, nor any thing that is thy neighbour's.*

Q. What is the sum of the ten commandments which is given us in the New Testament ?

A. The sum of the ten commandments is, thou shalt love the Lord thy God with all thy heart, and thou shalt love thy neighbour as thyself.

Q. What do you mean by loving God with all your heart ?

A. To love God with all my heart, is to have the highest and best thoughts of him, to desire his favour above all things, and delight to please him always.

Q. How must you shew your love to God ?

A. By paying him constantly the worship that he requires of me—by doing heartily whatsoever else he commands me—by bearing patiently what he suffers to befal me.

Q. What worship doth God require of you ?

A. I must hearken diligently to his holy word, and praise him for his greatness and goodness : I must pray to him daily for what mercies I want, and give him thanks for what I receive.

Q. And what do you mean by loving your neighbour as yourself?

11

"A. To love my neighbour as myself, is to do to all other persons as I could reasonably desire them to do to me, if I were in their place.

Q. *How must you shew your love to your neighbour?*

A. By honouring and obeying those that are set over me; by speaking the truth and dealing honestly with all who are about me; by wishing well and doing good to all mankind, whether they be friends, strangers, or enemies.

Q. *You have told me the duties you must do; can you tell me also the sins you must avoid?*

A. I must avoid all the sins of the heart, the sins of the tongue, and the sinful actions of life.

Q. *What are the sins of the heart?*

A. The sins of the heart are these, a neglect of God, pride and stubbornness, malice and envy, with all other evil thoughts and unruly passions.

Q. *What are the chief sins of the tongue?*

A. The chief sins of the tongue are swearing, cursing, abusing the name of God or any thing that is holy, scoffing, and calling ill names, lying and filthy speaking.

Q. *What are those sinful actions which you must avoid?*

A. Sinful actions are such as these, gluttony, drunkenness, and quarrelling, wanton carriage and misspending of time, especially the Lord's Day, doing dishonour to God or injury to man.

Q. *Have you never broke the commands of God, and sinned against him?*

A. My own heart and conscience tell me that I have broke God's holy commandments, and sinned against him, both in thought, word, and deed.

Q. How do you know that you have sinned in thought, word, and deed, against the blessed God?

A. I have let evil thoughts run too much in my mind, and spoken too many evil words; I have too often done such deeds as are evil, and neglected what is good.

Q. Whence comes it to pass that you have been such a sinner?

A. I was born into the world with inclinations to that which is evil, and I have too much followed these inclinations all my life.

Q. How came you to be born with such an inclination to evil?

A. All mankind are born in sin; because they come from Adam, the first man who sinned against God.

Q. But why did you follow these evil inclinations? was it not your duty to resist them, when you knew they were evil?

A. I ought to resist every sinful inclination, and therefore I have no sufficient excuse for myself before the great God.

Q. What do you deserve because of your sins?

A. My sins have deserved the wrath and curse of the Almighty God who made me.

Q. Is the wrath of God so terrible that you cannot bear it?

A. The wrath of God is terrible indeed, for he can make sinners suffer all the miseries of this life, the pains of death, and the torments of hell for ever.

Q. *How do you hope to escape God's wrath?*

A. God is merciful, and has sent Jesus Christ into this world, to become the Saviour of sinful creatures, as the Gospel teaches us.

Q. *What is the Gospel?*

A. The Gospel is the glad tidings of the way of salvation by Jesus Christ, which was foretold in the Old Testament, but is plainly revealed in the New.

Q. *Who is Jesus Christ?*

A. Jesus Christ is the Son of God, who was with God before the world was made, but he became the son of man, and dwelt with men about eighteen hundred years ago.

Q. *But is not Jesus Christ God, as well as man?*

A. Though he be a man, yet he is God also; for he is a glorious Person, in whom God and man are joined together, and his name is Emmanuel, or, God with us.

Q. *What did Jesus Christ do on earth to save sinners?*

A. He made known to men the will of God by his preaching; he set them a pattern of holiness by his own practice; he obtained pardon of sin and everlasting life for them, by his obedience unto death.

2

Q. How could Christ obtain pardon and life for us, by his doing or suffering?

A. Our sins had deserved death, but Christ was the Son of God, and perfectly righteous, and God appointed him to suffer death, to take away our sins, and to bring us into his favour.

Q. Is Jesus Christ now among the dead?

A. No: he arose from the dead on the third day, and afterward went up to heaven to dwell at the right hand of God.

Q. What is Christ now doing in heaven?

A. He pleads with God his Father to bestow mercy on men, and he rules over all things for the good of his people.

Q. What must you do to become one of his people, and to partake of this mercy?

A. I must repent of my sins, and confess them before God, and ask pardon for them; I must have faith in Christ as my Saviour, and obey him as my Lord and ruler.

Q. What is it to repent of sin?

A. To repent of my sins, is to be sorry at my heart that I have offended God, to hate every thing that displeases him, and to take heed that I offend him no more.

Q. What is it to have faith in Christ as your Saviour?

A. To have faith in Christ, as my Saviour, is to believe that Christ is the Saviour of sinners, and to give myself up to him, and trust in him, that he may save me in his own way.

Q. What reason have you to hope that you shall then be delivered from the anger of God?

A. If we repent of sin and trust in Christ, God hath told us in his word, that he will forgive our sins and save our souls.

Q. But is not your heart itself sinful, and have *you power of yourself to repent of sin, and to trust* *in Christ and obey him?*

A. We have sinful hearts and cannot do these duties of ourselves, but God has promised his Holy Spirit if we pray for it, to renew our hearts to holiness, and help us to do his will.

Q. How must you offer up your prayer, so as to *be accepted of God, and obtain his Holy Spirit,* *or any blessing from him?*

A. In all our prayers and all our services, we must seek for acceptance only from the mercy of God and for the sake of Christ; for we have sinned and deserve no good thing.

Q. Hath God provided any other means for *our help in the way to Heaven?*

A. God hath given his holy word both to Jews and Christians, he hath sent his ministers to help us to understand his word, and appointed some special signs and tokens of his mercy for our use.

Q. What are the special signs and tokens *which God hath appointed to shew forth his mercy* *among Christians?*

A. There are two signs or tokens, which are commonly called sacraments of the New Testament, and these are Baptism and the Lord's Supper.

Q. What is Baptism?

A. It is a washing with water, in the name of the Father, the Son, and the Holy Spirit.

Q. What is meant by this washing?

A. It signifies our being cleansed from sin, and our becoming new creatures and the disciples of Christ.

Q. Why must we be baptized in the name of the Father?

A. Because it was God, the Father of our Lord Jesus Christ, who appointed this salvation, and he is our Father also, if we are true Christians.

Q. Why must we be baptized in the name of the Son of God?

A. Because this salvation was preached by the Son of God as our great Prophet, he procured it for us as our High Priest, and he bestows it on us as our Lord and King.

Q. Why must it be done also in the name of the Holy Spirit?

A. Because the wondrous works of the Holy Spirit bore witness to this salvation heretofore; and it is this Holy Spirit enables us to obey the Gospel now, and to hope and wait for this salvation.

Q. What doth this Baptism in the name of the Father, Son, and Holy Spirit, oblige you to do?

A. If I am baptized, I am given up to the Father, the Son, and the Holy Spirit, that I may live as a new creature and a Christian; and having been once washed, I must not defile myself again with sin.

Q. *What is the Lord's Supper?*

A. It is the eating of bread and drinking of wine, in remembrance of the death of our Lord Jesus Christ.

Q. *What doth the bread signify?*

A. The bread when it is broken, signifies the body of Christ, which was wounded or broken on the cross for us.

Q. *What doth the wine signify?*

A. The wine poured out into the cup, signifies the blood of Christ, which was poured out in his death to take away our sins.

Q. *Why must the bread be eaten and the wine be drank?*

A. To signify our partaking of the blessings which Christ hath obtained for us by his death.

Q. *What doth the Lord's Supper oblige us to?*

A. Those who partake of the Lord's Supper, should thankfully remember the love of Christ who died for them, and they should love and serve him to the end of their lives.

Q. *When you have done the will of God, and served Christ to the end of your life, what are your hopes after death?*

2 *

A. When my body dies, and my soul goes into the world of spirits, I hope it will dwell with God and Christ, and be happy.

Q. And do you not expect some greater happiness afterward?

A. Yes; I hope for complete happiness when my body shall rise again, and be joined to my spirit at the day of judgment.

Q. But let us hear first what is this world of spirits you speak of, whither the soul goes at death?

A. It is a very large world, though it is out of sight, in which there are different dwellings, for angels and devils, and for the souls of men both good and bad.

Q. Who or what are angels?

A. They are good spirits, who wait on God and worship him in heaven, but they are often sent down to do service here on earth.

Q. Who or what are devils?

A. They are evil spirits, who were at first angels of God, but having sinned against him, they were cast out of heaven, and now they are always tempting men to sin.

Q. But are not all these spirits, both good and evil, put under the dominion of Christ?

A. Christ is Lord over them all: He employs the angels for the good of his people; and the devils can do no mischief, but when Christ suffers them.

Q. What will become of the devils at last?

A. They are now kept as prisoners for some greater punishment, after the judgment day.

Q. *When will this day of judgment come, when you said your body should rise from the dead?*

A. At the end of the world, Jesus Christ shall come down from heaven to judge all mankind, and for that purpose he shall raise all that are dead to life again.

Q. *What shall be done to mankind when the dead are raised to life?*

A. Christ shall call them all to appear before his seat of judgment, where both the righteous and the wicked must give an account to him of their behaviour in this world.

Q. *How will the righteous appear in that day?*

A. The righteous shall appear with courage and joy, as the children of God, who have done the will of their heavenly Father, and are made like him in holiness.

Q. *And how will the wicked appear then?*

A. The wicked shall stand before the Judge, with fear and shame, like the children of the devil: for they have done his will, and are like him in sinful works.

Q. *And how will Christ, the judge, dispose of men and deal with them in judgment?*

A. He will place the righteous at his right hand, and the wicked on his left, and will pass a sentence on them both, according as their works have been.

Q. *After the judgment, what shall become of the wicked?*

A. The wicked shall be driven into hell-fire, both soul and body, to be tormented with the devil and wicked spirits for ever.

Q. *And what shall be done to the righteous?*

A. The Lord Jesus Christ shall carry the righteous up with him to heaven, both soul and body, to live there with God their Father, and with his holy angels, in everlasting joy.—AMEN.

Hymns and Spiritual Songs.

The All-Seeing God.

ALMIGHTY GOD, thy piercing eye
  Strikes thro' the shades of night,
And our most secret actions lie
  All open to thy sight.

There's not a sin that we commit,
  Nor wicked word we say,
But in thy dreadful book 'tis writ,
  Against the judgment day.

And must the crimes that I have done,
  Be read and published there,
Be all exposed before the Son,
  While men and angels hear?

Lord at thy feet asham'd I lie,
  Upwards I dare not look';
Pardon my sins before I die,
  And blot them from thy book.

Remember all the dying pains
  That my Redeemer felt,
And let his blood wash out my stains,
  And answer for my guilt.

O may I now for ever fear
  T' indulge a sinful thought,
Since the great God can see and hear,
  And writes down every fault.

Thoughts on God and Death.

THERE is a God that reigns above,
  Lord of the heav'n, and earth, and seas,
I fear his wrath, I ask his love,
  And with my lips I sing his praise.

There is a law which he has writ,
  To teach us all that we must do,
My soul to his commands submit,
  For they are holy, just and true.

There is a Gospel of rich grace,
  Whence sinners all their comforts draw,
Lord, I repent, and seek thy face,
  For I have often broke thy law.

There is an hour when I must die,
  Nor do I know how soon 'twill come;
A thousand children young as I,
  Are call'd by death to hear their doom.

Let me improve the hours I have,
  Before the day of grace is fled:
There's no repentance in the grave,
  Nor pardon offer'd to the dead.

Just as a tree cut down, that fell
  To north or southward, there it lies:
So man departs to heaven or hell,
  Fix'd in a state wherein he dies.

Heaven and Hell.

THERE is beyond the sky,
  A heaven of joy and love,
And holy children when they die,
  Go to the world above.

There is a dreadful hell,
  And everlasting pains,
Where sinners must with devils dwell
  In darkness, fire, and chains.

Can such a wretch as I
  Escape this cursed end?
And may I hope whene'er I die,
  I shall to heaven ascend?

Then will I read and pray,
   While I have life and breath;
Lest I should be cut off to-day,
   And sent t' eternal death.

The Advantages of Early Religion.

HAPPY's the child whose youngest years
   Receive instructions well:
Who hates the sinner's path, and fears
   The road that leads to hell.

When we devote our youth to God,
   'Tis pleasing in his eyes;
A flower when offered in the bud
   Is no vain sacrifice.

'Tis easier work, when we begin
   To fear the Lord betimes;
While sinners that grow old in sin,
   Are harden'd in their crimes.

'Twill save us from a thousand snares,
   To mind religion young;
Grace will preserve our following years,
   And make our virtue strong.

To thee, Almighty God, to thee
   Our childhood we resign;
'Twill please us to look back and see
   That our whole lives are thine.

Let the sweet work of prayer and praise,
   Employ my youngest breath;
Thus I'm prepared for longer days,
   Or fit for early death.

The Danger of Delay.

WHY should I say 'tis yet too soon
   To seek for heav'n, or think of death:
A flower may fade before 'tis noon,
   And I this day may lose my breath.

If this rebellious heart of mine,
  Despise the gracious calls of heaven
I may be harden'd in my sin,
  And never have repentance given.

What if the Lord grow wroth and swear,
  (While I refuse to read or pray,)
That he'll refuse to lend an ear
  To all my groans, another day!

What if his dreadful anger burn,
  While I refuse his offer'd grace,
And all his love to fury turn,
  And strike me dead upon the place.

'Tis dang'rous to provoke a God;
  His power and vengeance none can tell;
The stroke of his Almighty rod
  Shall send young sinners quick to hell.

Then 'twill for ever be in vain
  To cry for pardon and for grace,
To wish I had my time again,
  Or hope to see my Maker's face.

Examples of Early Piety.

WHAT blest examples do I find
  Wrote in the word of truth;
Of children that began to mind
  Religion in their youth.

Jesus who reigns above the sky,
  And keeps the world in awe,
Was once a child as young as I,
  And kept his Father's law.

At twelve years old he talk'd with men,
  (The Jews all wondering stand,)
Yet he obey'd his mother then,
  And came at her command.

Children a sweet Hosanna sung,
  And blest their Saviour's name;

And gave him honour with their tongues,
   While scribes and priests blaspheme.

Samuel the child was wean'd and brought
   To wait upon the Lord;
Young Timothy betimes was taught
   To know his holy word.

Then why should I so long delay
   What others learn so soon?
I would not pass another day,
   Without this work begun.

Against Lying.

O 'TIS a lovely thing for youth
   To walk betimes in wisdom's way,
To fear a lie, to speak the truth,
   That we may trust to all they say.

But liars we can never trust,
   Tho' they should speak the thing that's true,
And he that does one fault at first,
   And lies to hide it, makes it two.

Have we not known, nor heard, nor read,
   How God abhors deceit and wrong?
How Ananias was struck dead,
   Caught with a lie upon his tongue?

So did his wife Sapphira die,
   When she came in and grew so bold,
As to confirm that wicked lie,
   That just before her husband told.

The Lord delights in them that speak
   The words of truth; but ev'ry liar,
Must have his portion in the lake
   That burns with brimstone and with fire.

Then let me always watch my lips,
   Lest I be struck to death and hell:
Since God a book of reckoning keeps,
   For every lie that children tell.

Against Quarrelling and Fighting.

LET dogs delight to bark and bite,
  For God has made them so;
Let bears and lions growl and fight,
  For 'tis their nature too.

But children you should never let
  Such angry passions rise;
Your little hands were never made
  To tear each other's eyes.

Let love thro' all your actions run,
  And all your words be mild,
Live like the blessed Virgin's Son,
  That sweet and lovely child.

His soul was gentle as a lamb,
  And as his stature grew,
He grew in favour both with man,
  And God his Father too.

Now Lord of all he reigns above,
  And from his heavenly throne,
He sees what children dwell in love,
  And marks them for his own.

—◦◦◦—

Love between Brothers and Sisters.

WHATEVER brawls disturb the street,
  There should be peace at home;
Where sisters dwell and brothers meet,
  Quarrels should never come.

Birds in their little nests agree;
  And 'tis a shameful sight,
When children of one family
  Fall out and chide and fight.

Hard names at first and threat'ning words,
  That are but noisy breath,
May grow to clubs and naked swords,
  To murder and to death.

The devil tempts one mother's son
 To rage against another ;
So wicked Cain was hurried on
 Till he had kill'd his brother.

The wise will make their anger cool,
 At least before 'tis night ;
But in the bosom of a fool
 It burns till morning light.

Pardon, O Lord, our childish rage,
 Our little brawls remove ;
That as we grow to riper age,
 Our hearts may be all love.

———◦◆◦———

Against Scoffing and calling Names.

Our tongues were made to bless the Lord,
 And not speak ill of men ;
When others give a railing word,
 We must not rail again.

Cross words and angry names, require
 To be chastis'd at school ;
And he's in danger of hell-fire,
 That calls his brother fool.

But lips that dare be so profane,
 To mock and jeer and scoff
At holy things or holy men,
 The Lord shall cut them off.

When children in their wanton play
 Serv'd old Elisha so,
And bid the prophet go his way,
 " *Go up, thou bald-head, go.*"

God quickly stopt their wicked breath,
 And sent two raging bears,
That tore them limb from limb to death
 With blood and groans and tears.

Great God, how terrible art thou,
 To sinners ne'er so young !

Grant me thy grace, and teach me how
    To tame and rule my tongue.

Against swearing, and cursing, and taking God's
*   name in vain.*

ANGELS that high in glory dwell,
    Adore thy name, Almighty God,
And devils tremble down in hell,
    Beneath the terrors of thy rod.

And yet how wicked children dare
    Abuse thy dreadful glorious name!
And when they're angry, how they swear,
    And curse their fellows and blaspheme!

How will they stand before thy face,
    Who treated thee with such disdain,
While thou shalt doom them to a place
    Of everlasting fire and pain?

Then never shall one cooling drop
    To quench their burning tongues be giv'n;
But I will praise thee here, and hope
    Thus to employ my tongue in heav'n.

My heart shall be in pain to hear,
    Wretches affront the Lord above;
'Tis the great God whose power I fear,
    That heav'nly Father whom I love.

If my companions grow profane,
    I'll leave their friendship, when I hear
Young sinners take thy name in vain,
    And learn to curse and learn to swear.

Obedience to Parents.

LET children that would fear the Lord,
    Hear what their teachers say,
With reverence meet their parent's word,
    And with delight obey.

Have we not heard what dreadful plagues
  Are threatened by the Lord,
To him that breaks his father's law,
  Or mocks his mother's word?

What heavy guilt upon him lies!
  How cursed is his name!
The ravens shall pick out his eyes,
  And eagles eat the same.

But those that worship God, and give
  Their parents honour due,
Here on this earth they long shall live,
  And live hereafter too.

———⊙⊷———

An Evening Song.

AND now another day is gone,
  I'll sing my Maker's praise;
My comforts every hour make known
  His providence and grace.

But how my childhood runs to waste!
  My sins how great their sum!
Lord give me pardon for the past,
  And strength for days to come.

I lay my body down to sleep,
  Let angels guard my head;
And thro' the hours of darkness keep
  Their watch about my bed.

With cheerful heart I close my eyes,
  Since thou wilt not remove;
And in the morning let me rise,
  Rejoicing in thy love.

3 *

A SLIGHT SPECIMEN OF MORAL SONGS.

The Sluggard.

'TIs the voice of the Sluggard, I hear him com-
plain,
You have wak'd me too soon, I must slumber again.
As the door on the hinges, so he on his bed,
Turns his sides and his shoulders, and his heavy
head.

A little more sleep, a little more slumber,
Thus he wastes half his days, and his hours with-
out number,
And when he gets up, he sits folding his hands,
Or walks about saunt'ring, or trifling he stands.

I pass'd by his garden, I saw the wild brier,
The thorn and the thistle grow broader and
higher,
The clothes that are on him are turning to rags,
And his money still wastes, till he starves, or he
begs.

I made him a visit, still hoping to find
He had took better care for improving his mind.
He told me his dreams, talk'd of eating and
drinking:
But he scarce reads his Bible, and never loves
thinking.

Said I in my heart, *here's a lesson for me ;*
That man's but a picture of what I might be.

But thanks to my friends' for their care in my
    breeding,
Who taught me betimes to love working and
    reading.

Innocent Play.

ABROAD in the meadows to see the young lambs,
Run sporting about by the side of their dams,
   With fleeces so clean and so white:
Or a nest of young doves in a large open cage,
When they play all in love, without anger or
    rage,
   How much may we learn by the sight.

If we had been ducks we might dabble in mud;
Or dogs, we might play till it ended in blood,
   So foul and so fierce are their natures;
But Thomas and William, and such pretty
    names,
Should be cleanly and harmless as doves, or as
    lambs,
   Those lovely sweet innocent creatures.

Not a thing that we do, nor a word that we say,
Should injure another in jesting or play,
   For he's still in earnest that's hurt:
How rude are the boys that throw pebbles and
    mire,
There's none but a mad-man will fling about
    fire,
  And tell you, *'Tis all but in sport.*

PRAYERS.

—◆◆◆—

A PRAYER

Proper to be repeated by a School, either Morning or Evening.

O God, thou art our God, we will praise thee: Thou art our Father's God, and we will extol thy name. Who is a God like unto thee, glorious in holiness, fearful in praises, doing wonders? The heavens and the earth are the workmanship of thy hands; and thou governest the universe in infinite wisdom.— Thou madest us for thyself, to show forth thy praise. But we are sinners: Thou madest man upright, but he hath sought out many inventions. We acknowledge that we were born in sin, and that in our lives we have wandered far from thy testimonies; for we have indulged evil thoughts, spoken evil words, and too often done such deeds as are evil.— Have mercy upon us, O our God; pardon our iniquities, for the sake of Jesus Christ who died for us, and deliver us from the wrath to come.—Lord, give us a new nature. Let Jesus Christ be formed in our souls the hope of glory.—Lord Jesus thou hast encouraged little children to come unto thee, and hast said, that of such is the kingdom of God. Lord, we would come unto thee. Take us in the arms of thy love and bless us, even us, and make us faithful subjects of thy kingdom.— O give us grace, we pray thee, to redeem us from all iniquity, and particularly from the sins and follies to which childhood and youth are subject. Give us a wise and an understanding heart, that we may know and do thy will in all things.—Be thou our Father; teach us and guide us, provide for us and protect us; and as we increase in years, so may we increase in knowledge and in a ready obedience to all thy righteous will. Train us up for usefulness in life: and when we shall have finished our days on earth, may we be prepared for death, and received to thyself in glory. May it please thee to hear our supplication for all mankind; especially for the sick, the sorrowful, and the needy. Grant thy blessings, we pray thee, spiritual and temporal, on our dear parents and other relatives and connexions in life. Bless all schools and seminaries of learning, and may this school be under thy special care and guidance. Assist us in our literary pursuits, dispose our minds to order and good government, and enable us diligently to improve the time and opportunities we enjoy, in such a manner as will hereafter render us useful to ourselves and to society.— Accept our thanks, O our God, for life and health, for food and raiment, for education, and for all the blessings of this life ; but more especially for the gift of a Saviour to a ruined world, the means of grace and hopes of glory. —Hear us and accept of us for the sake of Jesus Christ our only Saviour, and thine shall be the praise, Father, Son, and Holy Ghost, now and for ever.—*Amen.*

A MORNING PRAYER.

GRACIOUS God, I have been protected from evil through the past night, I have slept in safety under the shadow of thy wings, and been brought in comfortable circumstances to see the light of another day—for these and all thy mercies, I return thee my most sincere and grateful thanks.—Be with me, I beseech thee, through this day, preserve me from harm by thy power, supply my wants of thine abundant fulness, guide me by thy wisdom, and save me from youthful follies, by the influences of thy spirit.—Help me to remember that thine eye is upon me, that thou knowest my thoughts, my words, and actions, and that the day is at hand when I shall be judged before thine awful tribunal. Grant, O Lord, that I may never one moment forget that sin would destroy my peace in this world, would subject me to thy righteous displeasure, and blast all my hopes of everlasting salvation.— All which I humbly pray for, in the name and as a disciple of Jesus Christ.—*Amen.*

AN EVENING PRAYER.

Most adorable and merciful Heavenly Father, I rejoice in thy goodness by which I have been brought in safety to the conclusion of this day.—On thee I ever depend, who art the author of all my mercies. Save me, I entreat thee, from the baseness and the danger of making thee an unworthy return for thy blessings; if I have taken thy name in vain; if I have departed from the truth: if I have been undutiful to my parents; if I have kept bad company, or transgressed any of thy holy laws, Oh! forgive me I beseech thee, and grant that I may do so no more. Help me by thine aid to abstain from sin, to correct my follies, and as I advance in age, to grow in the practice of piety and virtue.—Keep me from evil, O Lord, through the silent watches of the night, favour me with refreshing sleep, and bring me in health and strength to see the light of the following day. Hear my prayers, I beseech thee, through Jesus Christ, and to thy name be everlasting praise.—*Amen.*

THE LORD'S PRAYER.

Our Father which art in heaven, hallowed be thy name. Thy kingdom come. Thy will be done on earth, as it is in heaven. Give us this day our daily bread. And forgive us our trespasses, as we forgive those who trespass against us. And lead us not into temptation; but deliver us from evil: for thine is the kingdom, and the power, and the glory, for ever.—AMEN.

—o◆o—

THE CREED.

I BELIEVE in God the Father, Almighty Maker of heaven and earth: and in Jesus Christ his only Son our Lord. Who was conceived by the Holy Ghost, born of the Virgin Mary, suffered under Pontius Pilate, was crucified, dead, and buried: He descended into hell; the third day he rose from the dead; he ascended into heaven, and sitteth at the right hand of God the Father almighty; from thence he shall come to judge both the quick and the dead. I believe in the Holy Ghost; the Holy Catholic Church: the communion of saints; the forgiveness of sins; the resurrection of the body; and the life everlasting.—AMEN.

FINIS.

CPSIA information can be obtained
at www.ICGtesting.com
Printed in the USA
BVHW05s0008030818
523375BV00013B/192/P